SNOW ON THE BACKS OF ANIMALS

Laurie Gibson Rayner
aug. 13, 1986

SNOW ON THE BACKS OF ANIMALS

POEMS BY

DAN GERBER

WINN BOOKS

SEATTLE

1986

ACKNOWLEDGMENTS

Some of the poems in this book appeared originally in the following periodicals: Pequod, The Wisconsin Review, The Nebraska Review, Poetry Now, Passages North, Red Cedar Review, waves, The Wayne Review, Corona, Contact II, Green River Review, Fireweed, X: A Journal of the Arts, Zero, Seizure, Puerto Del Sol, Elkhorn Review, Grey's Sporting Journal, The Small Towner, and West Michigan Magazine. Some of the poems also appeared in the following anthologies: *Yearbook of American Poetry* (Monitor), *Heartland* (Northern Illinois University Press), *Poems for the Dead* (Best Cellar Press), *Tigris & Euphrates* (X Press), and *Poets A to Z* (Swallow/Ohio University Press). "In the Winter Dark" was originally published in The Georgia Review. "Love For Instance," "January," and "Snow on the Backs of Animals" were originally published in New Letters. "Tathagata" originally appeared in The Chariton Review, and "Evening in Bangkok" appeared originally in Secret Destinations (Pequod 19/20).

ISBN 0–916947–08–4

Winn Books, *Publishers*
5700 Sixth Avenue South   Post Office Box 80096
Seattle, Washington 98108

PRINTED IN THE UNITED STATES OF AMERICA

1 3 5 7 6 4 2

TO THE MEMORY OF MY FATHER
AND TO WENDIE, FRANK, & TAMARA

Books by Dan Gerber

The poet judges, not as the judge judges
but as the sun falling around a helpless thing.
—WALT WHITMAN

One of his thoughts is the same as a blade
of grass or one tree because there is only
one life and one death.
—DOGEN [1244]

CONTENTS

[CONTENTS, *continued*]

SNOW ON THE BACKS OF ANIMALS

Dreams. Waking to snow falling in that
half-life, threads of the unconscious trailing
into the day as this late autumn snow
drifts down from the branches in the wind.
A little new snow falls into the yet
unfrozen water and dissolves like these
stories of my darker self, my more elusive
twin who, when I listen, has at heart
only my wellbeing.

A golden-eye dives through the dark mirror
of the pond. I reach back for you, my
friends, my selves who remain in the pillow,
in the crater where my head lay
replicating in a dozen disguises.

The door half open
in a dark hallway, rollerskate
on the stairs, marbles
scattered on the kitchen floor,
hold those impenetrable silences
between father and son
as the two drive home in the winter dark.

Do these smoldering logs, waiting
to be stirred back to flame,
become the compulsion to build cathedrals,
pyramids, tombs,
the great buried silos of North Dakota?

The shadow of a man trudges over the field.

One of those logs in the fireplace
suddenly takes off on its own
burning furiously
through a pocket of air.

The light fails so early.
The hemlocks grow heavy.

The shadow drives an image of the man before it.

It is early December and ice
has formed again on the lake.
I sit and watch the twilight
fade away without notice
like a widow who has outlived
her sympathy.

At dusk, I leave the cabin.
It is 1928, twelve years
before I am born. What have I to fear?
Coolidge is president, and America sleeps
its gleeful Rotarian dream.

Already the horses have gathered by the barn
and the burro stands way off braying.
I hear someone call my name
and turn,
but it's only the cat
come down from the hayloft
to ruffle his fur in the wind.

Tomorrow afternoon
we will carry these books to the basement.
Tomorrow afternoon we will burn the tree.
We will devise new ways
to protect us from our friends
and a list of everything
about which it is forbidden to worry.

I have opened the window.
The cold wind drives us to sleep.
Tomorrow we will face a continuing life,
consider grief a practical reality,
death a robber of pleasure,
this bed a preview,
the fate of our children,
the last bath, the last meal, the last click.

Tomorrow
we will have forgotten,
afraid something we might have said
would make a difference.

At the edge of the woods, I take off my skis and
sit back against a tree, enjoying the midwinter
sun. The sky, a blue bowl after weeks of grey
and listless snow. All day now I've been watched,
an intruder, lumbering through the dark trees. I
look but can't see the eyes watching me. I give
myself to the warmth on my face. I close my eyes,
awaken to the blood of my eyelids and see fiery
eruptions on the surface of the sun. I am still,
and the watchers come closer, uncertain I'm not
some kind of deep-blue fungus growing on the tree.
Soon I can see through their eyes, many eyes all
together, and through the eyes of the hawk turning
above, a white spot against the sky, a blue spot
against the snow, borne away by some instinct
from this thing I have been.

The loves of my friends are dropping like leaves,
each day a diminished affection.
The dust mote in a sunstreaked room
through which someone has passed.
The flurry of air behind them.

Morning, and the dream
steals away like those particles of dusk
in the early light.

A southeast wind is blowing
and the trick of time stills.
A far stand of pines, roaring like the sea.

And your mind becomes those minds you have loved,
not resting,
but fluid the way a dolphin swims
through ever changing galaxies
of krill and plankton.

SPEAKING TO HORSES

for Bill Dickinson

From my childhood I remember achingly clear winter
nights on the hay of a sledge, riding up snow-
covered country roads, singing, shouting, jumping
off and running alongside to impress the girls,
and under it all, the groundtone of his voice gentling
the horses. And I remember the sight of him across
our north pasture, following his team, the reins
across his shoulders, one foot in the furrow and
one on the newly turned ridge, like an ancient
traveler in our time, pursuing a life technology
and economics had declared defunct. But not for
him. He refused to be part of that progress-driven
consensus in its race for prosperity and oblivion.
For him, the horses were huge muscular children
who sometimes needed a firm hand, but never an
angry one, a life in the present, of caring and
slow time.

Two weeks ago, pneumonia ganged up with a
rare blood disease, and he died. There was standing
room only at his funeral, farmers in suspenders,
their weather-browned necks confined in white collars,
and many people my own age who must also, as children,
have heard him talking to his horses and learned
something about patience and gentleness. Outside,
a team of Belgians, the horses of a friend, stood
harnessed to a black box-carriage in the hot September
sun. Occasionally they pawed the pavement and
nuzzled each other as befit the occasion in their
being horses. Two drivers in black livery and
tophats with black sashes waited to take him on
his last carriage ride. Traffic backed up all
through town as the procession moved with the same
mindful slowness with which he'd lived.

Up ahead, as the carriage turned down the
cemetery lane, we could see the giant horses ambling
through the shadows of the trees.

RETURN

I

September, and the acorns come crashing
from branch to branch, whistling through the leaves,
all around the dark house
like tiny planets cast out from space.
Not an hour goes by but I wonder
at the weight of sadness that pulls them down.
I kindle the first fire
and pull up my chair and sit close.

A blind man, they say,
can smell the night coming on.

II

Autumn moans through the cabin door,
sounding of winter and darkness and sleep
and something more certain.
In the north wind,
the lake flows south like a river
past an opening in the trees.
I watch it for hours, drifting
through huddled fields and creaking woods,
past empty farms
where armies have camped and moved on.

Then Black Hectcin, to relieve the burden
of his timeless dark, reached down to the mud
and fashioned a creature and spun it, and the
mud bird dreaming the Earth in its giddy whirl
struck off stars, rabbits, fire, willows, even
the bird of its dream became actual, and as
the spinning slowed, took the first wobbly
step on the first touch of land and teetering
back on its tail, conceived the sky for balance
and the sun for the father of shadows.

And the dreambird imagined feathers to justify
the rush of its wings and, lifting over
the now-appearing hemlocks, grass fields to
join them and the mirror of lakes to appease
the sky, and in its first tentative maneuvers,
drunk with the glory of its vision as it dipped
low among the hills of its wavering flight,
dreamed a creature who looked up, who stumbled
in amazement and called out its name.

GENERATION

Do I want my children to be little
me's, grieving every real
or speculated grief?
Lost on long solitary walks
in the snow,
thinking nothing and thinking
about that too?

EVENING IN BANGKOK

The perimeters of light behind Wat Pho,
the longboats working upriver,
and flower girls, not twelve years old,
emerge in the traffic with fragrant strands,
bell-like and pungent as gardenias,
in hands more delicate and eyes
black as prayer.
Garlands sewn by their keepers
to embrace a wrist
or dangle from a rearview mirror,
adorn the Buddha on the dash.

The light changes.
You buy her flowers.
You're moving now.
You want to give her something more,
perhaps to say *forgive me*.

He wanders into the November fog
disturbed by a picture in the catalogue,
the tight stretch of white silk
over that fullness where the legs become one.
And he's certain that triangular shadow
wasn't just a play of studio light
but a woman who may, at this very moment,
having forgotten about the photograph,
clipped, pasted in her scrapbook and labeled
"Me," be musing over her morning cup,
steam rising against the dun light, wondering
if he, though she doesn't know his name,
will appear at her door, his hair damp,
his face and shoulders coated with fog.

My hands fly away in the darkness,
a dream filled with strangers.

Outside the wind drives snow against the window
through the roar of darkness and empty trees.

I pull the door shut behind me,
take refuge in the barn,
and linger among the cows
clinking in their stanchions.

Somewhere in the night, maybe
even within this present storm,
a woman seeks an image resembling mine
among these hearts and this steaming straw,
the pungence of fermenting corn.

I latch the door again
and bear these bones back toward the house,
a matrix and a destiny,
like any bit of cosmos.

The old horse walks to the edge of the
pasture and stands stretching his neck
over the fence, as if he could see through
the falling snow, smell the ungrazed
grass matted under the ice or the frozen
orchard across the road.

There is no color in the earth or sky.
Viewing his world so long from this ground,
he knows the past and future as a windmill,
a tractor, a pump arm that beckons.

DECEMBER

Night has been falling all afternoon.
I'm not concerned with what comes or goes.

Below my feet
snakes coil together.
Not one bird is flying.
Not one fish cares about ice.

The last flies buzz,
slow and clumsy.
They stumble across my knuckles
and I let them.

They are old and the year is old,
and I haven't lived
a more perfect day.

Driving past on a winter evening in his old Desoto
with my father, the dark windows of the second
story stared out like the faces of prisoners.
"Someday you'll take me there," my mother would
say, half in jest. The Poor Farm, everyone called
it, and I wondered what kind of badness would put
someone there, behind the brick walls and icy windows
of that gaunt place in the empty fields. "You
grow old," my father said, "with no money, no family,"
an anteroom for death, he called it. I snuggled
close, the heater of the Desoto whirring at my
feet against the crimes of poverty and age.

Now a new building sprawls over the fields,
like an insurance office or junior high, with thermo-
pane windows, lawns, now buried in snow, and a paved
drive I cross to visit Aunt Hattie, not really my
aunt, but closer, who told me Tom Thumb stories
while she scrubbed my ears and kept the ghosts
away while my parents were gone. "I'm gonna run away,"
she says, playing the child. "I'll run to your house."

Her roommate lies curled in the corner, staring
at things only she can see. Her eyes shed my greeting
and my words stumble back as they do at a party
when you're telling a story and realize no one
is listening. Hattie's eyes look up from the bed.
"I'm awful tired," she says, and I kiss her. She
tells me, as she always does, what a fine man my
father was, how neither I nor my grandfather could
ever hope to match him. "But you're okay," she
adds, "You were all good kids."

"How old are you now, Hattie?" I know this
already, but it makes conversation. "I'll be 87
next June," she says, "but I don't care if I make
it." I tell her again of my children, growing
up and leaving home. "Big stuff," she says. "It
don't hardly seem possible. Big stuff."

The woman down the hall is screaming, as she
does every day, a mindless Morse code, and the odor
of a bedpan drifts into the room. We get used
to it, or it fades, I'm never sure which. An anteroom
for death, my father said. "They treat me okay,"
she says. "The Lord know where I am."

I promise to come again when I kiss her goodbye,
wishing for a moment I could roll my life back
up into that Desoto, dragging her with me, and drive
on toward home. From the cab of my truck, I look
back at those windows, glad my father isn't there
to see me driving away.

I please myself not answering the phone,
not caring who called.

Wind carries the lake past my window
like a river, *interminably flowing.*

And nothing stops, nothing
ends here.

Later I will go and tell the burgher
a story to amuse the inquisition.

The way is so long
it doesn't bear thinking about.
You'll go mad if you try to figure it out.
The owl puffs up his feathers against the cold,
and the hemlocks droop under the heavy snow.
But they don't break.
It is only another winter.

You return home
to find your house no longer there.
The trees have grown back
and the toe of a boot you received for Christmas
protrudes through the loam of your floor.
The door you locked in the morning
is the space between twilight
and the serialized stars,
and your wife and children,
their wings extended,
circle the treetops
and sing indifferently of what you were.

He wasn't permitted inside
but would stand out in the yard
among the towering oaks
and wave to his father at the window.
They would wave to each other
until it seemed silly, like saying
"door" a hundred times.

Then suddenly his father would be gone
and he would find himself
waving at the black window, feeling foolish,
hoping no one was watching
the fluttering of his hand
like a bird in the air at his side.

Where the sun rests we rest from its light.
But not in time.
We rest in the dream of darkness,
no further than our eyelids,
no further than life from death ever strays,
or death from life.

LEGEND

When his face looked back at him
from the covers of too many magazines,
his dog wandered off and skulked in the trees.
Old friends called,
but there wasn't time to see them anymore.
Everything was moving so fast,
and the woman
in whom he'd so often found solitude
seemed shabby now, and besides,
he belonged to the world and Orson Welles,
and when, in desperation, he took that long walk
around his neighbor's pasture,
he turned back halfway,
unable to go on, having nowhere to go.

THE ONE INSIDE

Inside the window
is the maker of the house,
and inside the basket,
the great weaver.

In the thread, the spinner
spins out his life,
and in the stone my mind caresses,
the Earth does its slow beginningless work.

A spring wind rattles the window,
and the farmer turns fitfully under the moon.

Tubers sprout below the frostline.
Soon the fields will be plowed.

What snow is left whitens the gullies
like sweeps of canvas waiting for paint.

I awake and my parents are together again
as if they'd discovered that death was a dream.

Last night as I stopped at a crossroads, a pickup
sped past, and in my headlights I saw something
horrible, a dog being dragged by its neck, skidding
over the pavement like a broken toy. A mile down
the road I pulled the truck over. "You're dragging
a dead dog," I shouted. He was an old man with
wild hair and thick glasses. The sticker on his
bumper said, *Happiness Is Knowing You're Going To
Heaven.* The dog was torn open, the bones and membrane
of its shoulder exposed, its paws bloody where it
must've tried to keep up with the dumb force dragging
it into the dark. "I couldn't feel nothin' " the
man said. "I don't even like dogs. This rig's
been my home for three years. I travel around
preaching the gospel."

And then I saw the dog was still alive, a pup
not more than six months. It lay quiet, like a
good dog, and I stroked its ears. I didn't want
to see the other side, the side underneath where
its body met the road. Its eyes followed my hands
as I reached down with my pocket knife and cut the
cord from its neck. "Somebody musta tied it there,"
the man said. "I musta dragged it three miles."

Later the sheriff came. "Didn't you know he was there?" He was looking at me, and I knew how he felt. "It isn't my truck," I said. "Why don't you put him away?" I stroked the dog's ears one more time. I wanted him to know some tenderness. "Gentlemen, please step aside." The sheriff drew his gun. I turned away as he fired, again and then again. The dog kicked spasmodically, rolled on its back and howled, the only sound I heard him make, like a woman crying over a child. "Aw come on," the sheriff pleaded. "Don't make me do it again." He fired once more. The dog's legs took one final stride against the sky, its eyes glowed in the headlights, and a last breath steamed out against the cold night air. I pulled him off on the grass by the road, pulled him by his ears and tail, all I could grasp that wasn't bloody. "The road crew'll get him tomorrow," the sheriff said. "I drive around," the man said. "I couldn't keep a dog in there."

The grass and small flowers bear my tread
like the slightly bruised lips of a lover.

Hair on the pillow, wild hair
like grass in May. The new green

leaves on their limbs, a dress
that shades the darkness of her thighs,

wherein to lay my head. Apple blossoms
and dust blow over the yard.

JOURNAL ENTRY

Though supposedly spring,
snow is falling for the third straight day.

Two weeks ago my father died,
and I'm with him now
more than when he was living.
I see him with my grandparents,
thinner,
in a white linen suit and Panama hat.
He dances with my mother
or stands in the back of a Model T truck,
in his uniform, just back from France.

Then, sitting on his knee,
unjustly spanked,
my lips protrude, and my skin
forms a cauliflower of rage.

I follow him like an old black dog.
Yabut, he calls me.
Yeah, but, I say, *but it isn't fair.*

I feel the cold
through the soles of my shoes,
the peepers sing from the pond,
a few more flakes in the air.

It's the moon's sadness or the sadness of
cranes, standing all night, one-legged, over
the still pond, or just the silhouette of
rocks on the water, the heart of which has
been invaded by a single thought, and though
unmoving, grows restless as the blood of the
outwardly placid man. Later, near the cold
dawn, a vapor rises, pulling down the sliver
of light, and the birds begin a chorus, neither
greeting nor farewell.

A man struck by lightning
is seldom appeased by house current.
The bolt that steals vision or
restores it, splits the young poplar,
hurls thunder over the roof,
makes widows of farm wives
and ashes of the barn.

The wild geese never die; the lilacs
reappear each May, and the night sky
continues its imperturbable dance.

In Bruckner's 4th, someone is hunting on the
far side of a mountain lake. Soon the hunt
is abandoned for the mysteries of the forest,
a small pond, an opening in the earth for
the sky to flow through, where the hunter
lies down in long grass.

The dark is so thick I spread my arms and
swim toward the surface of light. It envelopes
my skin, the exact temperature of blood, calls
to the dark man within me. There is nothing
of which I am not. The wind rises, and my
wings, rushing all day over the fascinations
of Earth, find a break in the trees and begin
their slow, joyful circling into night.

It wasn't as it might've been had it rained.
I would've sat in the Cuban bar drinking coffee,

watching the people in the street getting wet
and not caring.

I wouldn't care, and they wouldn't care.
I want you to understand.

At this latitude rain, by itself, doesn't matter.
It comes like sweat,

and dries in its own good time.
People die or leave town,

and nothing changes but the moon
and what the tide brings in, bright men-of-war,

oily bubbles a child might've blown,
a suitcase full of sand, a lawnchair,

anything the Earth might offer you. Three girls
lying topless, six breasts pooling into themselves.

Six perfect nipples, two hard as buttons,
two peaked like pink custard,
two dark as knots in varnished pine.

Voices begin to flutter
like the wings of a frantic bird,
so much to be said
the room will not hold them,
so much talk of love,
the word is finally a mouthful of dough,
love love love love love.
Now bang your head on your lover's knee,
bang bang bang bang bang,
and tell me
what's the difference.

He dreams of her head thrown back on the pillow,
her cries of relief from so much longing.

Her breasts slope to him,
a valley leading home,

no longer aware
of being a man or a woman,

only blood on the snow,
and a bird is flying.

I am walking at the edge of town
when, through the uncut grass at the bottom of a hill,
I see an old garage, long neglected,
doors rotting on their hinges
and no tracks leading to them.
Inside, after prying the doors apart,
a black car, a limousine, still shiny,
and, side by side as if returning from the opera,
the deliquescent bodies of a man and a woman,
their evening clothes still elegant,
sag into the mohair seat.
I place a daisy in his lapel,
pin a black-eyed Susan to her dress.
The doors resist me as I force them apart,
pushing my shoulders through the water of sleep.

Voices through the wall.
I hear myself taking each part,
my wife, my daughter.
The dog barks at a stranger,
waiting for the hair on his spine to lie down,
for the chance to speak my lines,
to explain this intrusion.

Suddenly I feel uneasy.
The dog goes on barking.
The girl seems frightened.
The woman simply stares.
I have forgotten my excuse
and avert my eyes,
confronting the man
I am about to become.

He scans the negatives
of breasts and knees and tangled hair,
his own face demonic
in reversed light.
He becomes the girl
entwined with this stranger,
unsure of himself
as she falls back on the sheets,
surrendering,
as if to a syringe filled
with unknown dreams.

I lived in a house
where it rained every day
and the wind played middle C
on the windows.

She was the only woman alive
for miles
and I forgot there were things to be done.

I don't remember the first time
I went there
or the last time I closed the door.

She said she was going for the groceries,
and when the wind stopped,
I was gone.

Someone is watching,
even in this basement room
with the door locked and the one
small window covered,
someone is watching, even
when I turn out the lights
and walk into the swamp,
up to my knees in the muck,
miles from any road,
someone is watching, getting dizzy
with the velocity of my dreams
but hanging on
to the idea of watching,
even though now there is
no one to watch.

She said I was sweet,
to gall her husband,
humping against me as we danced.

The house was surrounded by poison ivy,
in the dark, in the sand,
the summer lightning and wind,
a delicious idea
kept safe in the house.

I am what is left
of last night's whiskey,
all that remains of that woman,
a trace still left in the ashes.
That which hasn't burned
attracts fire.

I sat without moving
for over an hour.
The pain in my legs
had come and gone.
My desire for her had
come and gone,
become only desire,
and miles away in the morning,
someone was using a chainsaw
to clear trees
brought down by the storm.

I adjust the dial and bury my head in the stream,
concentrating on the beat of rain
to wash away all expectations
of what you will be. I lather my hair,
my face, neck, arms, every crevice
and contour. The water bears down, soap
swirls on the drain as you slip
between sheets, humming your impatient song,
pondering what didn't get done, is the cat out
and did you turn the sprinklers off?
I watch the whirlpool and dry my hair.
Are you thinking of me? The drain croaks.
I focus on my breath.
You turn to look at the moon.
I towel my back and thighs, imagining your breasts,
your sculptured throat. You feel a tinge of sleep
warming around you as I enter the bed,
pretending I'm another man.

All this happened when I was ten.
I have no one to blame but myself.
She said she'd give her life for me.
What would I do with it?
"I have all the lives I can use.
Here, take one.
No, you choose, any one you like.
They spoil so quickly in this weather."

She said she would show me my soul.

I found her at the circus.
She cleaned the tiger's cage,
then slept in it.
Soon she will sleep in the tiger.
She said she liked his eyes.
She wanted to see them from the other side.

Chaff gets down my shirt, and the cut stalks of
the bale ends rub my forearms raw. Always the
hottest day of the summer, always, with clouds
getting dark in the west, when the wagon is borrowed
to haul hay from Monette's. We used to put up
our own, but farming's an expensive hobby. The
elevator rigged to the loft of the barn, the wagon
hitched to the truck, and every year the same
reminiscence, work and wages now, compared to when
we were young, though I went to school with Monette's
daughter, and his youth and mine were in different
worlds. "Kids don't want to work that hard anymore,
no matter what you pay," he says. "They ain't got
the patience." But for Monette and me it's easier
now, past the agony of feeling our lives getting
away from us. We develop a rhythm, building the
load, knowing that though the years seem short,
the day is long, and there's nowhere else to be.

My daughter, Tamara, pulls the bales from
the rick, and Monette and I heave them up to Warren
who interlocks the rows. We try to keep count
but get lost and have to refigure it, a hundred
on the wagon, fifty on the truck. Two loads should
hold us the winter. A dollar-fifty a bale this
summer; he could get three if he held it til the
snow comes, but that's not his game he tells us.
"Turned down a man from Indiana, wanted five thousand
bales just like that." He snaps his fingers, then
wipes the sweat with his sleeve. "But it's a one
time deal. I got to service my regular customers."

48

It's nearly mid-afternoon when I pay Monette
and we pull out slow, gentling the load down his
drive. We take our time. Once Warren and I dumped
half a wagon on Main Street and had to rebuild
it in blocked traffic and unwelcome advice from
the sidewalk. Play-farmers exposed. We turn the
vent windows all the way round, hoping to find
something cool in the air. Our shirts stick to
our backs, and the heat slows down in our heads.
Tamara has a crush on Warren and teases him about
his girlfriends, testing this new woman beginning
to take over her name. She slugs him on the shoulder
as a sign of affection, and then, to be democratic,
ruffles my hair.

In the loft, Warren and I strain to keep pace
with the bales Tamara and her brother, Frank, feed
the elevator. The heat up here throbs like a drum.
The elevator's clatter pushes us on. I catch the
bales and pitch them to Warren in what becomes
a machine-like dance. We keep space for air between
the bales and the wall. Barns have exploded in
heat like this. We keep space around the windows
and keep them open. Sweat gets in our eyes, and
our throats ache with the dust and chaff. For days
we'll find fragments in our navels and ears. The
loft shrinks as the hay closes in around us.

Finally, I turn for a bale that isn't there
and look down and see that the wagon is cleared.
My son and daughter are bombarding each other with
the broken leaves. Warren and I wonder at their
energy as we collapse on the mound we have built,

feeling righteous and empty. I recall something
Thoreau said, that nothing is so unprofitable as
talking with farmers because they always fall back
on their virtue. Maybe so. If I were to speak
now I'd say something like, "Yes, the Earth is
good," and so I keep silent. "The Man who pretends
to be a modest enquirer into the truth of a self-
evident thing is a Knave," Blake said. I laugh
at the way other men's words dribble out of me.
Warren thinks I'm laughing at our transformation
into hayseeds, at the straw he's poked up his nose,
and we laugh together over that and our agreement
about how easy a few cold beers will go down. We
hear the first rumble of thunder in the west. I
feel the stiffness already in my shoulders as I
get up and walk to the hay door. At the far end
of the pasture the horses graze, their noses deep
in the succulent grass.

The dream of a sheepdog, torn by its comrades,
widows with scrapbooks of ships lost at sea.
We waited in the village more than a week,
sipping tea in stone rooms with leaded windows.
The barber away with his mother in the north
while his half-witted apprentice fondled the razors.
Overhead, an airplane soared in search of its engine
while storms wracked the coast with urchins and spume.

I finger the beechnuts, already falling, and
the late blackberries along the path down
to the lake where the maples are turning
red. I look at them a long time and don't
think about my life.

We found ourselves on the inland sea.
Over the city, the smoke in a solid plane
erased the tops of buildings,
and evening sank like a distant gong.

The lives of farmers and taverns
entered the night of a prairie
by the light of freeways
where a few dogs bark,
beyond rivers and catfish
that float on the dew of thick grasses.

And over a million vague salesmen
high on quotas
and a million solid citizens
buying guns
and a million schemes of sad barbers,

the mountains rise and the planets move
with the grave logic of their lives.

There are Indian mounds, two or three,
said to border this lake,
but I haven't found them,
rain that fills the trees,
earth that holds them spongy,
remnants of ancient barbed wire
grown halfway through their trunks.

In winter it seems a frozen pasture.
Only its flatness and irregular shape
would make you suspect
that under the snow, there's more.

Except for a silo on the hill
above the trees on the western shore,
almost obscured by leaves,
or a jet dividing the sky
at noon,
the Indians, one hundred years
before Christ, had yet
to build their mounds.

Birds feed and die at its edge,
herons nesting in tamarack,
a snake crawls into the nest
or dangles from the claw of a hawk,
the soft aggressive slither,
the heron gliding at sunset.

This spring, two horses drowned,
great children plunging
through the fluted ice,
the splash and struggle;
the broken water reforms,
clouds part, the sun appears,
a kingfisher flies low
and rattles out his call.

I drift in my boat
with no story,
connected to nothing but the shore.

Wind flues in the pines overhead,
dapples the face of the water,
alters my line
as I cast to small fish,
dreaming
on beds of old leaves.

And catch the image of the fisherman,
no more observer than observed,
no more observed than rings
pooling at the exposed roots
of the maple where a life has risen
to dance with the bones of my wrist.

Just now I have entered the sinewy world of
shoulders. Shoulders of the Bahamian woman
on the pier where the fishermen bring turtles
to die on their backs as slowly as
they would crawl across a small city.

Under the cool of her dress, her bones range
as finely as a sparrow's wing.
The last day of August, it is cool as September.
A cool east wind chills the dew on the grass;
my shoulders hunch in their sleeves.

Just now I thought of the Bahamian woman
and the ease of her bones on that pier.

THE LINE

A day worth losing
flows by with the river.

The brown skin of my hand
turns over a line,
gathers slack from the current.

Each day there are messages
we ignore by the stream.

The line moves
as stars flow,
in patterns a life goes by.

No song, but in my ear,
lead, fire, rain,
tar and couch grass,
the picture in a million grey dots.

The lines of my hand
flow off the edge,
rivers of the world
irretrievably lost,

      discipline   discipline
channeling my life
in the music of the world.

I have opened this line
to the threads of a milkpod,
spunk smell of loam,
effulgence of the brain,
the idle lust of my eyes.

SASSAFRAS

Now that frost has returned
and numbed the mosquito,
I go back to the trail I cleared last year
and find you have retaken it,
your odd fingered leaves
defending what I'd laid bare.

I set to work with my knife again,
slashing right and left till the air is ripe
with your scent and mine,
two armies contending this ground,
and may neither one of us win.

The smoke of burning leaves intoxicates the
sleepy towns of the recession. Another autumn,
no good news, and winter storms coming on.
He rocks on his porch, not unconcerned, but
what is there to be done? He can't clear-
cut the yard to stoke an oilstove or bale
his lawn for the dog. His measure and level
languish in the hall. He starts awake with
an aimless joy, bearing from sleep the heft
of a hammer rocking in the bones of his hand,
the last nail-thud alive in his ear. The
clean scream of his saw fades off down the
street, and he isn't quite sure whose street
this is. His wife's been riding his nerves.
He's sleeping later every day, and his lunch
pail gapes at the kitchen wall, a small tug
far from the sea.

You could no more force it
than you could stop it from coming.
The lamp sputters and fills the house
with the smell of oil.
I look at the moon but don't see it.
For days,
aware of nothing,
I've been watching my mind,
watching my mind,
watching my mind.

Hunters parade through town,
deer strapped to their fenders.
I suggest to my friends
we strap each other to fenders
and drive through town,
dress cows up in flannel cow suits,
wear masks of our own faces.

I turn and walk into the mirror,
another room in which nothing has changed.

SURVIVORS

Maybe it's late on a Sunday afternoon when
you stop to watch ice forming around the one
red leaf that floats on the pond, and you
wonder if you've been a success and from whose
point of view. Or maybe you're buoyed up
on good news, fearing the inevitable fall,
when you see someone you believed had been
dead for years, and she pretends you don't exist.

Remember the first time you held her hand
in the flickering light of the silver
screen, how you waited til the horseman had
rescued the girl and then, as if in relief,
reached out, how your lips seemed to cling
a moment longer than you intended as you pulled
back from a kiss.

Remember the newsreel footage of the accident,
the twisted metal, the thought of what remained.

Or maybe you married years ago, and you look
again, and there is no leaf on the pond.

FLY

Again moving over the page as I read,
you stop and rub your legs together
as if having come across something juicy,
or maybe it's only a configuration of type
that resembles something you love,
this capital M, your own wings.

You climb the knuckles of this hand
that whisks you away and would
smash you if it were quick enough.

You work the edge of the paper
as if wanting to see the next page,
then return to the M of Mortality
as long as the book remains open.

What is there in this life
that puts a wall between us
and the moon borne over the windy night,
through which we have forgotten the dead
who held us and the frail clouds
and the new snow barely touching
the downed leaves,

like a man who holds his wife at arm's length,
observing her under the light,
and weeps for his loss of passion?

2:00 A.M.

This pen in my fingers,
making heroes and villains
with a few strokes of black ink,
now trees, horses, women in love and women
wanting to be in love, wanting to be told
worlds, stars, clouds, melting ice,
the faces of strangers no longer strange
and of friends made strange with fear,
of wind, whispers of deception, thunder,
can you hear it now, wait,
it will come again, thunder,
prayers, ships passing unnoticed
and snow falling into itself.

Finally you are leery of all intentions,
those expectations that color the life
through which you see all this green Earth, stones,
flowers, doorways, benches and jugs, only
as fodder for the eye, and hear
in all the household gods
the strangled voice of self-judgment.

You avoid the dark places,
avoid being alone.
Desire and its attendant, fear,
sing to you from the glades of midsummer.

You dream of a fire or great wave
to sweep away all you own,
long for a mob of Tartars
to storm this wall of good sense
you've built around you like a tomb.

You are walking down a country road,
bored, and about to turn back
or in a city with the noise of buses
when your heart aches
for a life free of shops and schemes,
with nothing to protect you
from the voice in the whirlwind,
the language of salt,
the Ariadne who lives next door.

We say *tree*
for the object that isn't there.

We say *I love you*,
acknowledging the failure
of whatever there was
to speak for itself.

We say *God did it*;
we mistrust everything.

You read these lines.
You think of something profound.
You pay too much for the ticket
and miss the plane.

The wind abides nowhere.
Or it isn't the wind;
it is the motion of the mind
through pine boughs.

CANTICLE

I want to use the word
in a story, in a poem, in speech,
the ring of the chair on its axis,
the whir of the heater in my room,
the bell-like sound of this word,
saddles and candles and gongs,
chanting in the dome of the Taj Mahal,
my tongue rocks in its bed,
water in a subterranean pool,
sweet desire,
that draws me with its heat,
a fine distinction between this and that,
welded in a sound, bearing
the mind in its tone.

My father swerved to miss a paperboy, turned the
wrong way up a one-way street and got nailed by
the cop on the corner. He never had a chance to
explain, and it wouldn't have made any difference.
Maybe the cop had been pondering a nightmare, his
wife moaning under the dance instructor two floors
down or his daughter threatening to leave home
if she couldn't go up to Wisconsin for the weekend
with the defensive backfield and a couple of other
friends. It isn't easy being a father; I realize
that now, the long silent burns I caused, those
looks of resentment, ways I had of putting the
guilt on him. Maybe we're all that way, and he
was thinking about that when the newsboy stepped
off the curb to sell a paper, never intending to
dart into the street. "Where're you from, anyway?"
the cop yelled back, after the lecture, after telling
him to beat it. "Fremont," my father shouted,
feeling his small-town pride as he said it, certain
the cops in Fremont were never thus blind. "I
thought so!" The cop heaved his shoulders and
turned away in disgust. In every thought I've
had since he died, my father has forgiven me.

After the full moon, we awake
to discover the leaves have fallen.
Sunlight penetrates the fog
and a friend calls
in the desperation of living this everyday life.
The dog sleeps at the end of the couch,
and the log in the fire
hisses with last night's rain.
When I hold my hand to the sun
I can see the blood in my fingers.

*   *   *

To say that you are greater than the trees
because you move through them at will,
like a king through his retainers,
would be to say that you are
greater than your eyes or your fingers
or your mind.

A painter deprived of his sight,
or the darkness its dreams.

*　*　*

The dead may return to us as flowers,
not with human feelings
but as pure expression. They
may also inhabit the wind or
the sense of being we have,
alone sometimes, just before dark.

*　*　*

I bend down and touch
the greenest blade of grass.
It was easy to find,
like falling asleep a little drunk
and waking up in the morning.

ADUMBRATIO

In his death, my father has been wandering
through the forest. He enters a clearing
and stops to ponder the living sweep of the
sky. He holds back in the shadows, so as
not to be noticed, avoiding the probing fingers
of light. Sometimes he takes the form of
a bird or a pebble or the wind's high rejoinder
in the pines. When clouds build over the
afternoon, his shadow dissolves into moss,
lichen, the dry carpet of leaves. I walk
eastward along the bed of a stream where
a stream once was or will be.

This morning, before a strong south wind moved in
to clear the lake of winter, I saw a fox trying to
find his way off the ice, testing the edges,
retreating again and again until he found a spot
that would hold, that would get him back into the
forest.

A tree. A perfect tree. A large oak catching and
releasing the wind. A hundred years of life, a
thousand board feet that could become an ark, an
oak bridge, an armoire for a queen, but never
again a beautiful tree.

Is it possible the fox may be my father, returned
to innumerable lives, none of them better or worse
in the judgment of the fox, who chooses without
question whatever is given?

Should I save the frog from the snake gliding
toward the edge of the lake? Should I save the
sparrow from my cat, save the chicken from my
table, stewing in its broth of wine, tarragon and
garlic?

I can't save the deer. I start with each shot and
run to the window and realize what I hear is only
target practice or an orchard gun or at worst a

death quicker than by wild dogs or starvation. I can't save my friend from the cancer distending his liver or the woman who cared for me from the years that have worn her away, much less the starving of Africa to whom I send money or those in love with ignorance who will never open up to their lives.

Eleven years since my father died to the day I found a fox with his leg in a trap, waiting like someone's red dog to be unchained, until I got close. I pinned him down with a log and sprang him free as he snarled and bared his fangs at whatever it was that caused him pain. The trapper followed my tracks and threatened to kill me. "If that's what you've decided to do," I said, the .357 in his holster, the cold blue-black of a cobra at close range, and I desperately did not want to die.

Three beautiful skulls in my cabin: turtle skull, deer skull, long-horned steer, white and perfect structures on which no life can be rebuilt. Add to them the skull of the dog who sleeps on my couch, of the cat who sleeps on the rug at my feet, skull of the woman whose head rests on the pillow next to mine, the skull I feel with my fingers through my cheeks, so white and perfect and on which no life can be rebuilt.

There is a peacefulness
when snow falls like this, over everything,
and keeps on falling, windlessly,
on fence rails and ditches, made level now,
filling the upturned pail in the yard,
wiping the field clear of corn stubble, even
smothering the news and anyone
attempting to reach us.

A man walks out on a night like this
and the darkness weighs down his arms.
He forgets his purpose, stumbles,
gives up whatever it was he wanted
and enters the bodies of his friends,
growing deep and luminous.

Composed in Ehrhardt types
by Wilsted & Taylor, Oakland, California

Printed & bound by Braun-Brumfield, Inc.
Ann Arbor, Michigan

Designed by Scott Freutel
Langley, Washington